WITHDRAWN

Skiing for Beginners

Skiing for Beginners

by **BRUCE GAVETT,** Director
Haystack Ski School
and CONRAD BROWN

Skiers PETER MUMFORD
and CINDY GAVETT
photographed by KIM MASSIE

Charles Scribner's Sons
New York

Grateful acknowledgment is made to James A. Carroll, Jr., who originally suggested this book; to Haystack Mountain in Wilmington, Vermont, for the use of its facilities during photography; to certified instructors Ann Tumavicus and Charles Abarno for their help; to Irwin Frank, the knowledgeable proprietor of the Alpine Ski Shop in New York City, for guidance on equipment.

Photo page 15, courtesy Spinnerin Sports; Spinnerin skiwear styled by Gusti.

Copyright © 1971 Conrad Brown

This book published simultaneously in the United States of America and in Canada—Copyright under the Berne Convention

All rights reserved. No part of this book may be reproduced in any form without the permission of Charles Scribner's Sons.

A—8.71 [RZ]

Printed in the United States of America
Library of Congress Catalog Card Number 75-143921
SBN 684-12510-2

Contents

To the Parents of a Young Skier	7
To a Young Skier	9
Skis	11
Rentals	11
Boots	12
Bindings	13
Safety Straps	14
Poles	14
Glasses	14
Ski Clothing	15
Walking on Skis	17
The Sidestep	18
How to Get Set	19
Straight Running	21
The Straight Snowplow	22
The Herringbone	24
Exercise: The Snowplow Change-up	25
The Snowplow Turn	27
Linked Snowplow Turns	28
The Kick Turn	30
The Traverse Position	33
Exercise: Bobbing in a Traverse	36
Exercise: Stem-Traverse-Stem	37
The Stem Turn	38
The Forward Sideslip	40
Exercise: Traverse plus Forward Sideslip	42
Exercise: Stem to the Forward Sideslip	44
The Uphill Christie	46
The Snowplow Christie	49
Exercise: Stem Christie Garlands	51
Exercise: Beginning Stem Christie	52
The Stem Christie	55
Exercise: The Fan	57
The Parallel Christie	59
Exercise: Parallel Turn over a Bump	60
Parallel with Check	62
The Short Swing	64

To the Parents of a Young Skier

Skiing harnesses the natural derring-do that most children possess and directs it into the formation of such qualities as self-reliance, judgment, and initiative. Skiing is a fine character builder.

This book is for any youngster who can read well enough to understand it. The best age for beginning to ski depends very much on your child's temperament, physical development, coordination—and eagerness. There is no longer considered to be any lower age limit, although most children younger than six are not ready for serious instruction.

If you as a parent are a good skier, you can get your small child started on skis merely by having him play follow-the-leader with you. He will mimic whatever you do. A little child usually stands correctly over his skis if he is not told to "bend your knees." If he should stick out behind or lean over when he's skiing down, you need only suggest that he'll find it a lot easier if he stands naturally over his skis.

A good way to teach a small child how to make turns is to have him follow you as you turn on top of low bumps on the practice slope, having first taken him straight over the same easy bumps a few times. By this simple method most little children can attain some semblance of parallel skiing in a surprisingly short time.

Make it easy for your child to enjoy learning to ski. Start him off on skis no longer than his height and equipped with name-brand release bindings, which should be adjusted by a professional. See that he has boots that fit. This is important and need not be costly. Many communities across the snow country have set up family bartering facilities, so that children can trade in their boots for larger ones when they outgrow them. Your school's athletic department may be able to refer you to a swap-and-barter setup.

As your child begins to show aptitude for the sport, be sure and have him take lessons at a ski school that is a member of the Professional Ski Instructors of America and refer him to SKIING FOR BEGINNERS to help him comprehend the whys and wherefores of technique.

Any discussion of twisting the body on its axis is purposely eliminated from this text—no mention of "counter motion," "counter rotation," or "reverse"—for two good reasons: The concept is too difficult, in a book for children, to pile on top of all the other body motions asked of a beginner; and there appears to be a de-emphasis of rotation, both in ski schools and among racers.

To a Young Skier

Almost all of America's present ski racers learned to ski when they were very young, perhaps six or eight years old. If you are serious about learning to ski, it's a smart idea to learn good technique from the ground up as early in life as you can.

The American Ski Technique is your best choice. It is the system taught in most ski schools in this country. With it you will learn to make long, beautifully carved parallel turns and the tightly controlled short swing. With the American system you will learn to ski with confidence and style. It's not the shortest route to parallel skiing ever invented and it isn't particularly easy, but if you stick with it you will become a more thoroughly trained skier than by any other system.

This book provides a standardized series of steps that puts a solid foundation under your technique. It enables you to continue improving all the rest of your life. Anyone can learn to get down a slope on skis without learning the basics. But many a discouraged *poor* skier has found that, if he is to have any hope of becoming a *good* skier, he has to start all over—and it takes much longer to *un*learn bad habits.

Can you really learn to ski from this book? The answer is yes—but do not neglect any chance to take lessons at a ski school, preferably at one where the instructors wear a stars-and-stripes pin reading "Professional Ski Instructor of America." Here you will get reliable instruction like the instruction you find in this book.

Today more and more people learn to ski by GLM, the graduated-length method invented by ski instructor Clif Taylor. Kids have always enjoyed the advantages of GLM, starting on short skis and "graduating" to longer ones as they grow bigger. The American system's snowplow-through-parallel route continues to be best for anyone starting on long skis who prefers to go the one-length-of-ski route from beginner to expert.

You will find SKIING FOR BEGINNERS a good book to study both before and after any ski class or practice session to make sure you've got it all together—in your head, in your muscles, and in your reflexes. You can use it for review at the beginning of each ski season, going back over the all-important fundamentals as the first snow flies.

Study the pictures closely. They tell you far more about correct position of your body and of your skis than any long-winded description could ever do. If you follow the sequence of steps in SKIING FOR BEGINNERS faithfully and practice to perfect your skiing, you will in time experience the supreme thrill of swinging away down a mountain in a series of perfectly controlled turns, whipping up a sparkling plume of snow.

Skis

If you are a young skier who is still growing you can acquire all of your equipment oversize and grow into it—except for your skis. If you buy skis the proper height (no longer than you are tall) the first ski season and grow a lot, it won't matter if your skis are a little short for you by the following winter. They will simply be easier to handle.

Begin on plain wood skis. Watch out for secondhand wood skis, however. They may be warped without your being able to tell—you will merely be frustrated at how long it's taking you to learn to ski. Skis are very carefully designed to make skiing easier and surer. They have to have the right amount of camber, for example. This refers to the bow in the ski that raises its center point off the floor when you lay it down flat. If the camber has gone out of it or if the ski is twisted, you'll waste a lot of time on the practice slope. So begin your skiing on brand new skis if you can possibly afford them.

When you begin to ski well, even if you are only seven or eight, a switch to more expensive metal or fiberglas skis will make a tremendous instant improvement in your skiing because of their superior engineering and the livelier response that these modern materials make possible. If you ski often enough, there comes a time in your progress when metal or fiberglas skis are worth the difference—even if you have to work all summer to earn the money.

How stiff should skis be? The answer is, not stiff at all, unless you take up racing. By then you will know exactly what degree of stiffness suits you. Meanwhile, "standard" flexible skis make learning easier and swifter. Stay with them until you are really good.

Rentals

If you don't intend to ski more than a few days in the course of a ski season, particularly if you are still growing, renting ski equipment makes a lot of sense. Today all major ski areas rent excellent equipment. In the rental shop at the foot of the mountain you are likely to find a greater selection in sizes of boots, skis, and poles than in ski shops near your home. The trick is to get there early enough your first day of skiing to avoid having to wait in line and lose valuable time out on the slope while your bindings are being adjusted.

Boots

You ski with your body. Your boots transmit the actions of your body to your skis. This means that boots are vitally important to your chances of becoming a good skier. Quality plus fit equals control, faster and safer learning, comfort, warmth, and longer boot life. As a beginner, if you're growing fast, however, you should consider boots no more than one size bigger than a perfect fit. Try them on over one pair of heavy socks and fill them up with a second pair of heavy socks (but no more) to get a tight fit the first season on skis. The second season they will probably fit perfectly. As you begin skiing well you will want a more precise fit when you buy boots.

Ski boot in a release binding. The pictures below show how the binding releases the boot in the event of a spill. Note the safety strap attached to the boot and to the rear part of the binding. It keeps the ski from sailing off down the hill by itself if the skier comes out of the binding.

Modern ski boots are so tough there's little you have to do about maintenance beyond wiping them off after skiing. In cold weather, to ski with warm feet, it's a good idea to start out the day with warm boots. Take them indoors at night; don't leave them in the trunk of the car. Trying to warm up cold boots with your feet is a losing battle. Your feet will simply get colder and colder as the day progresses. Wear insulated socks—the ones known as "Hot Dogs" have a wicking action that draws the moisture away from your skin. On really bitter cold days some skiers find that silk socks under their heavy wool ones give added resistance to the cold.

Bindings

Let's face it—if you get hurt skiing you might lose out on a whole winter's fun. Your best protection against accidents is becoming a good skier. Experienced skiers who ski in control have far fewer accidents than poor skiers. The next best protection against accidents is properly adjusted release bindings. All bindings are release-type today, but not all are good bindings. The newer name-brand bindings made for juniors are safer than ever, however. Make your choice with the help of a professional at a ski specialty shop. He knows what is correct for you. The clerks in other stores may only pretend to know—and you need the very best help you can get when it comes to buying bindings, having them mounted on your skis, and getting them properly adjusted. Don't take unnecessary chances.

There is no sure way, in truth, for even an expert to size up your weight and degree of skill and set your bindings so that you are sure you will always come out of them in every spill and never come out of them while making turns down the slope. Have the ski shop adjust your bindings initially to the lightest possible setting for your weight. Then go out and try them at that setting, skiing very carefully, of course. If you come out of your bindings skiing normally, have them tightened just a bit and go back out and try them again. If you still pull out when you're skiing, have them tightened some more. This is the only way to get maximum safety from release bindings in a bad spill. It's worth the trouble not to be laid up with a bad sprain or a broken bone while your friends are out there having fun.

Safety Straps

There is one inexpensive item of equipment that all ski areas require you to use. It's a pair of short straps; one end of each strap attaches to the binding of your ski and the other end to the boot, so that if you come out of your bindings in a spill your skis will not go careening down the hill, a danger to every skier in their path. (Incidentally, if you ever see a ski doing that, yell SKI as loud as you can to warn other people to get out of the way.)

Poles

In any sport there are fads that come and go. In skiing the "proper" length of ski pole is something that seems to keep changing. One season a new racer will come to the fore using long poles, and everyone goes out and buys long ones. The next year it's short poles. Your best bet as a beginner is a moderate length, long enough to help you climb up the slope and get around on the flats but not so long that the poles get in your way when you're skiing down. Elbows in touching your sides and hands straight out from your elbows grasping the pole handle (at the ski shop, not in the snow), that's a reasonable length. As you improve you may want shorter or longer poles. With luck, you'll be able to trade.

Glasses

If you wear prescription lenses you will ski better with them than without them. You will be able to see subtle changes in the slope well before you get to them and adjust your position accordingly—but have your prescription ground in unbreakable plastic, and do purchase an elastic band that clamps tightly onto the ends of the bows of your glasses behind your ears, so that you will not lose them in the snow if you take a spill. There's no need to have your prescription ground in sunglasses. You can wear a colored plastic visor over your glasses when the sun is bright.

Ski goggles are good when you start skiing faster and especially if you start racing.

Ski Clothing

As a beginner you will probably find that you have dressed too warmly the first time you go skiing. Skiers have discovered that if they wear windproof outer clothing over a few layers of woolen clothing they can adjust the number of layers to the temperature of the day.

Warm-up suits are outer garments that cover you from neck to boot. Some have extra zippers running down the sides of the legs. They keep the coldest wind out when you're riding up on the chair lift and can be zipped open without having to be removed when you come inside for lunch. In fact, a warm-up suit may be all you need. On cold days wear long thermal underwear and just pull the warm-up suit on over your boots, pants, shirt and sweater, and you will be nice and comfortable. The greatest thing about warm-up suits is that they keep your legs warm. A warm leg skis better than a cold leg and is less likely to get its owner into accidents.

A knitted cap (buy it at a ski shop if you want the right kind) and good, warm leather mittens will take care of the parts of you that stick out of your warm-up suit, except in the very coldest weather such as Eastern skiers can expect. Then you may want a second pair of wool mittens to wear inside your leather ones, and a face mask. They're fun!

In warmer weather ski in jeans if you must—most kids do—but be aware that jeans are not very practical. Unless you have them waterproofed, they get soaking wet if you fall in wet snow.

Walking on Skis

The first day you put on your skis you should spend some time getting the feel of them. Stand on a perfectly level place, plant your poles in the snow, and lift up one ski. Swing the tip back and forth, then up and down. Lift the other ski and repeat the process. Try lifting the tails, one at a time.

Now, forgetting about the poles, begin walking ahead. The skis should stay in contact with the snow. You must not pick them up. They should glide along. If you have plenty of flat space, keep going and make a big circle.

What if you should happen to fall (now or later)? The easy way to get up quickly is to draw your feet well up under your rear. Then just roll sideways over your boots and stand up. That's all there is to it.

Now walk for a distance in a straight line. Try using your poles as if they were two canes, planting them close to your boots, left ski and right pole, right ski and left pole. At the end of your track *step* your skis around. Lift the tails to make the hands of a clock, as Peter is doing in the picture, and walk back again.

then I pick up the other ski and step it sideways up the hill.

and set it down, rolling it onto its uphill edge to make it hold . . .

Facing straight across the slope, I pick up one ski . . .

The Sidestep

The sidestep is the most reliable way to climb a hill. Use the sidestep for going up—or getting down—steep or difficult places. It's just like climbing stairs sideways. The left pole moves up with the left ski and the right pole with the right ski.

Study these pictures of Peter climbing by sidestepping and read his own explanation of what he is doing. Start with the bottom picture and read upward.

Sticking my ski poles in the snow down the hill, well away from my feet...

I lean my weight on the poles and step the tails around up the hill...

until I am pointed down. If it doesn't feel too steep, I just go—by picking up my poles, or...

How to Get Set

Rely on your ski poles to get in position to ski down. Stab both poles firmly into the snow downhill from your body, lean on them, elbows straight, then step the tails around uphill until you are pointed down. Now just pick up the poles and go.

if I decide I want to go slowly, I step the tails apart...

then I just lift my poles and go down in this position, keeping my skis quite flat on the snow.

19

Straight Running

Practice straight running first on an easy slope with a long flat runout at the bottom. Straight running is a natural, comfortable, relaxed position. The skis should be flat on the snow and quite close together. Let your arms hang loose, with your elbows flexed and your hands forward about the height of your hip bones, somewhat away from your body. Stand straight and flex your knees and body slightly forward. Flexed knees act as shock absorbers when you ski over bumps and through dips. Your body should form a right angle with your skis at all times, the way Peter's does in the picture on the facing page.

Weight evenly distributed, lean forward so you feel pressure on the entire soles of both feet. Above all, *don't sit back*. Instead, stand right over your skis so that you have the feeling, when you go, that *you* are taking *them* down the hill. They should never take you for a ride. Of course, when the going gets steeper you will have to tip a little farther forward from your ankles to keep your body perpendicular over your skis.

The Straight Snowplow

Correctly done, the snowplow will give you your first real feeling of control over your skis. It is used to stop at slow speeds, and it is also from this position that your first turn will be learned.

Try the straight snowplow on the flat area at the foot of the practice slope first. With tails apart and tips together, stand quite erect, then relax completely. Flex each knee forward toward the front of your skis. (The feeling is a bit like trying to kneel on the front of your skis.) Keep your rear in.

Now hop your skis together, then hop into snowplow position again. This is a good exercise for getting to know the snowplow.

Climb a short way up an easy slope near the bottom of a hill that has a flat runout. Get set (*as you learned on page 19*) by sticking your poles in the snow downhill from you and stepping the tails around until you are facing down the fall line in straight snowplow position . . .

What's the *fall line*? A term heard often in ski school, it is the line a ball would take if you carried it up and let it roll down the hill by itself . . .

Bending ankles forward, knees forward and keeping the hips forward as you move ahead, draw your knees toward each other just enough to make the skis brush lightly across the snow. If your skis tend to cross in front, it means that you are drawing your knees too closely together. To flatten your skis so that they gently brush the snow and slow your speed, first make sure your weight is evenly distributed on both skis, then pretend you are riding a fat horse. Snowplow to a gradual stop.

In these two views of the straight snowplow, front and back, notice that the skis are in a V at equal angles from an imaginary line drawn straight down the fall line. Tips are close together. The tails are comfortably apart—not too wide open. The lower leg is directly over the top of each ski. The hands are hip-bone high and the poles point back, out of the way. Weight is evenly distributed on both skis.

The Herringbone

The herringbone is the fastest but most tiring way of climbing up.

Try the herringbone without ski poles at first, transferring all of your weight back and forth from one ski to the other. Now try it using your poles. Push on the opposite pole each time you take a step. Where it gets steeper make a wider V with your skis, pressing your knees well forward in toward the hill in front of you so the edges of your skis will grip.

exercise:

The Snowplow Change-Up

Use the snowplow as a brake to go slowly down very easy slopes. Don't use it for making sudden stops. Think of the snowplow as a way to control your speed.

The snowplow change-up is an exercise that combines the straight snowplow and straight running. As you are moving downhill in a snowplow, draw your legs together to close the V until your skis are tracking side by side. As you continue moving ahead, sink slightly and brush the tails gently apart until you are again moving in a snowplow. Let the skis run together again, then put on the brakes—but gradually!

That's the snowplow change-up. Practice it all the way down the slope to get ready for what comes next.

I start down an easy slope in straight snowplow position.

When I am moving along comfortably in control...

I tilt my upper body out over one ski to see what happens...

I've made my first turn on skis!

The Snowplow Turn

When you can do a fairly well-controlled snowplow—and that means being able to snowplow slowly straight down a gradual hill with both skis evenly weighted—try an experiment: Transfer more weight to one ski than the other as you snowplow down and see what happens . . .

How do you transfer more weight to one ski? You tilt your upper body out over the ski . . .

It really works. The skis will turn. Try it to the left, then try it to the right. Don't rush the action. *Weight* one ski—then *wait* for the snowplow turn to happen.

Skiing across the slope in snowplow position...

Linked Snowplow Turns

When you can make snowplow turns to the left and to the right, try putting several together. Keep going. Make a snake. Do one snowplow turn after another on down the hill. Stay in snowplow position and simply tilt your upper body to transfer your weight out over whichever ski is pointed in the direction you want to turn next. This is the ski that becomes the *outside* ski of that turn.

As you begin a snowplow turn, keep your skis fairly flat, gently brushing the snow. Press forward the outside knee (the knee over the outside ski of the turn) as you tilt your upper body out over the outside ski.

Study the pictures. Each turn is completed by a steering action, with all the weight forward on the turning ski, and leverage coming from the knee. That's *how* it turns. Snow resistance against the weighted front part of the turning ski is *why* it turns.

If you have trouble completing your snowplow turns (which means continuing to turn until you are skiing across the hill in the new direction), try edging the outside ski inward just a bit after you pass the fall line. This will help you complete your turns, particularly when the snow is hard-packed or a bit icy.

Now I transfer my weight to my right ski and tilt my upper body out over the turning ski to make a turn to my left.

I transfer my weight to my left ski and tilt out over the turning ski . . .

to make a turn to my right.

After I have crossed the fall line, I press my downhill knee forward and roll that ski onto its edge so that I will keep crossing the hill.

You should really consider snowplow turns as an exercise—a step along the road to becoming a good skier. They are not to be used at any but the slowest speeds while you are learning to ski. Don't permit yourself to become a "snowplow expert" and invite accidents. The straight snowplow, with tails wide apart, is dangerous to use as a brake if you should get going too fast. Do NOT snowplow to try to stop if you do get going too fast—instead just sit down and slide to a stop. The only really safe way to ski fast is with your skis parallel, side by side like railroad tracks. We're coming to that.

See how my upper body tilts out over the weighted left ski as I begin a new right turn.

Plant poles.

Downhill ski up . . .

around . . .

and . . .

down.

The Kick Turn

You may not use it very often, but the kick turn is handy to know, even if it is a bit tricky. Practice it first on flat ground before you try it on a hill, as Cindy demonstrates here.

Jab the pole securely in the snow uphill and face downhill as you begin. As if you were kicking a football, swing your downhill ski up and set its tail in the snow. Then let it drop out around away from you and down. Set it firmly in the snow so it will stay in place. The other ski can now be brought around easily.

Uphill ski ...   *around ...*   *and down.*

The Traverse Position

The best way to get the idea of proper traverse position is to do a snowplow turn to a stop, with your downhill ski coming to rest across the slope *(bottom picture on facing page)*. Freeze in the snowplow that produced the turn. Now bring the uphill ski in alongside the downhill ski. Study the picture below. See how Peter's ankles, knees, and hips are flexed. Notice especially that his uphill ski is slightly ahead, his uphill hip is slightly ahead, and his uphill shoulder is slightly ahead. His weight is almost even on both skis, with a bit more weight on the downhill ski.

You are now looking at correct traverse position. You need to know the traverse position to get across steep slopes without sliding sideways. It's also the basic position at the end of every parallel turn. Correct traverse position is important. For another look, turn the page.

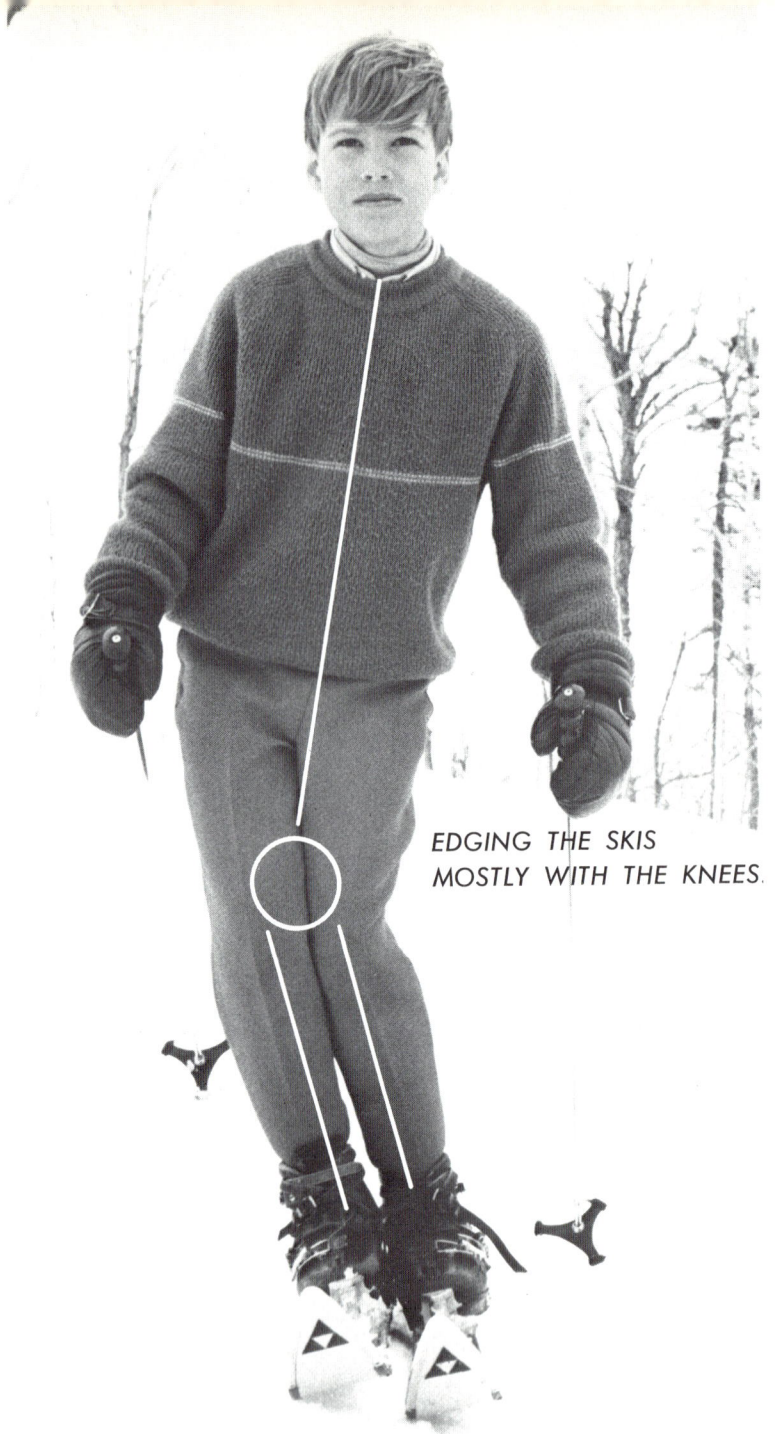

EDGING THE SKIS MOSTLY WITH THE KNEES.

This is how the traverse position looks straight on. Everything uphill is slightly ahead of everything downhill: uphill ski, uphill boot, uphill knee, uphill hip, uphill shoulder—all are slightly ahead.

The uphill edges of both skis are *set*. This means that they cut into the hill. You set your edges in the traverse position by keeping your knees in toward the hill. The upper body tilts out away from the hill. This puts more weight on the downhill ski, and that's just as it should be. The skis will cut a clean, sharp track in the snow and run side by side.

EDGING THE SKIS BY ANGULATION.

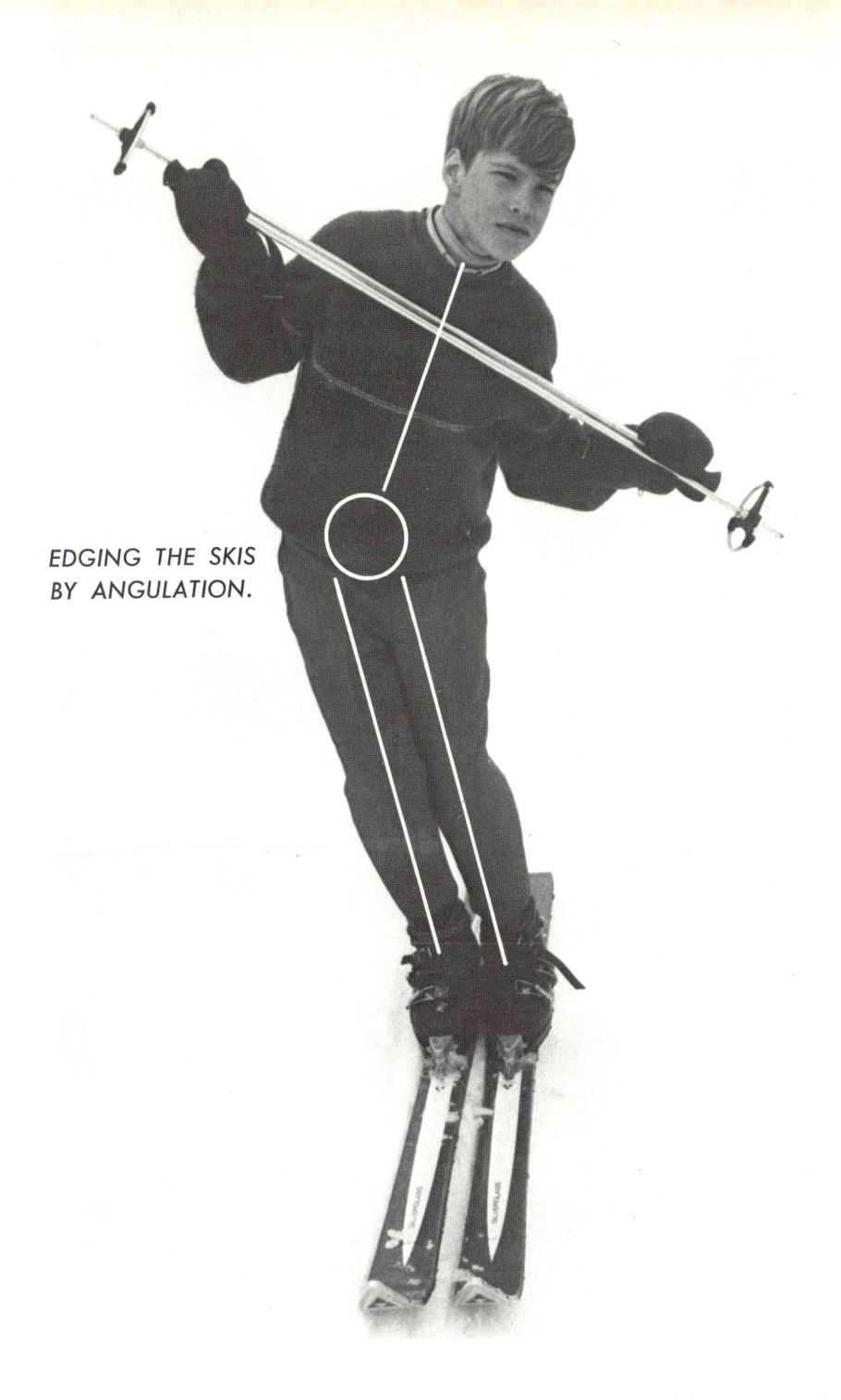

When you want to cross a really steep slope you will be surprised how easy it is, in the traverse position, if you are willing to make your upper body lean well downhill keeping your knees well in toward the snow beside you. As this picture demonstrates, the steeper the slope, the more you will need to angle your upper body out from the hill and push your knees into the hill. Peter has aligned his ski poles to demonstrate the increased steepness, meaning that an imaginary line through his shoulders would parallel the pitch of the terrain he is skiing on.

exercise:

Stem-Traverse-Stem

Here's another exercise you should do while you are practicing the traverse. It prepares you for the next step, the stem turn . . .

What does *stem* mean? When you open one ski in half a snowplow you *stem* that ski . . .

As you are traversing the slope, uphill ski slightly ahead, transfer all your weight to the downhill ski and stem the uphill ski. Brush its tail out smoothly, but do not weight the stemmed ski.

Stem and together, stem and together, that's how it goes. Play a game with yourself: See if you can make three stems with the uphill ski while tracking a perfectly straight line with the downhill (weighted) ski.

exercise:

Bobbing in a Traverse

Here's an exercise to help you learn to traverse a slope.

As you are crossing the hill completely relaxed—with your uphill ski, boot, hip and shoulder slightly ahead—merely sink down and forward with your entire body. Then rise—and sink down. Head up, watch where you are going, and don't look at your feet. Keep bobbing like this all the way across the slope.

Crossing the hill in traverse position...

The Stem Turn

Basically, the stem turn is a steered turn just like the snowplow turn, except that instead of stemming both skis as you did in the snowplow, only one ski forms a half-V—the uphill, *outside* ski of the turn.

Begin the stem turn in a traverse and end it in a traverse: As you are crossing the slope (skis parallel, "everything" uphill slight ahead), stem the uphill ski out. Smoothly and gradually transfer your weight onto that stemmed ski and continue around past the fall line as if you were making a snowplow turn. At the end of the turn, with a slight rise of your body, let the uphill ski glide in alongside and slightly ahead of your downhill ski. Continue in the new traverse direction.

Link several stem turns, with a few yards of traversing between each of them.

To come around more swiftly in a stem turn than you did when you were making snowplow turns, step firmly and forcefully onto the outside ski immediately after stemming it out. Faster stem turns are actually easier on steeper slopes, because the force of gravity helps pull you around. Once you are headed in the new direction, guide the uphill ski in smartly —and slightly ahead. Don't leave it out there in a half-V. Get into traverse position again.

Practice the stem turn not to perfect it but merely to get the hang of it, and go ahead with your learning. Follow Peter and Cindy through the next few pages as they prepare you for the real fun—parallel skiing.

*I rise slightly
as my unweighted uphill ski
glides smoothly in alongside
and somewhat ahead of my downhill ski.*

I stem the uphill ski out...

and transfer my weight to the stemmed ski.

The weighted outside ski steers me across the fall line...

and into the new traverse.

Skis rolled onto their edges grip the snow.

Flattened skis sideslip.

The Forward Sideslip

Unless you find a good, steep, smoothly packed slope, the sideslip is hard to learn. There are two reasons why it's vital that you practice this maneuver: One is that from now on all your turns (until you learn racing turns) will include a certain amount of controlled sideslip. The other reason is that knowing how to sideslip can come in handy on the mountain if you should come to a dropoff in a trail that's too steep for you to ski.

The pictures above show how the sideslip works. The skier is in the traverse position. He flattens his skis to make them begin sideslipping by moving his flexed knees *away* from the slope.

Peter shows you on the facing page how the forward sideslip is accomplished. As you are moving across the slope in a traverse, abruptly rise —with a *catlike* up-motion of your entire body—and flatten the skis. This releases the edges and enables the skis to slip forward and sideways at the same time. It's tricky and it takes practice, but sideslipping is worth it. On the next few pages are some sideslip exercises that will make learning to christie easier.

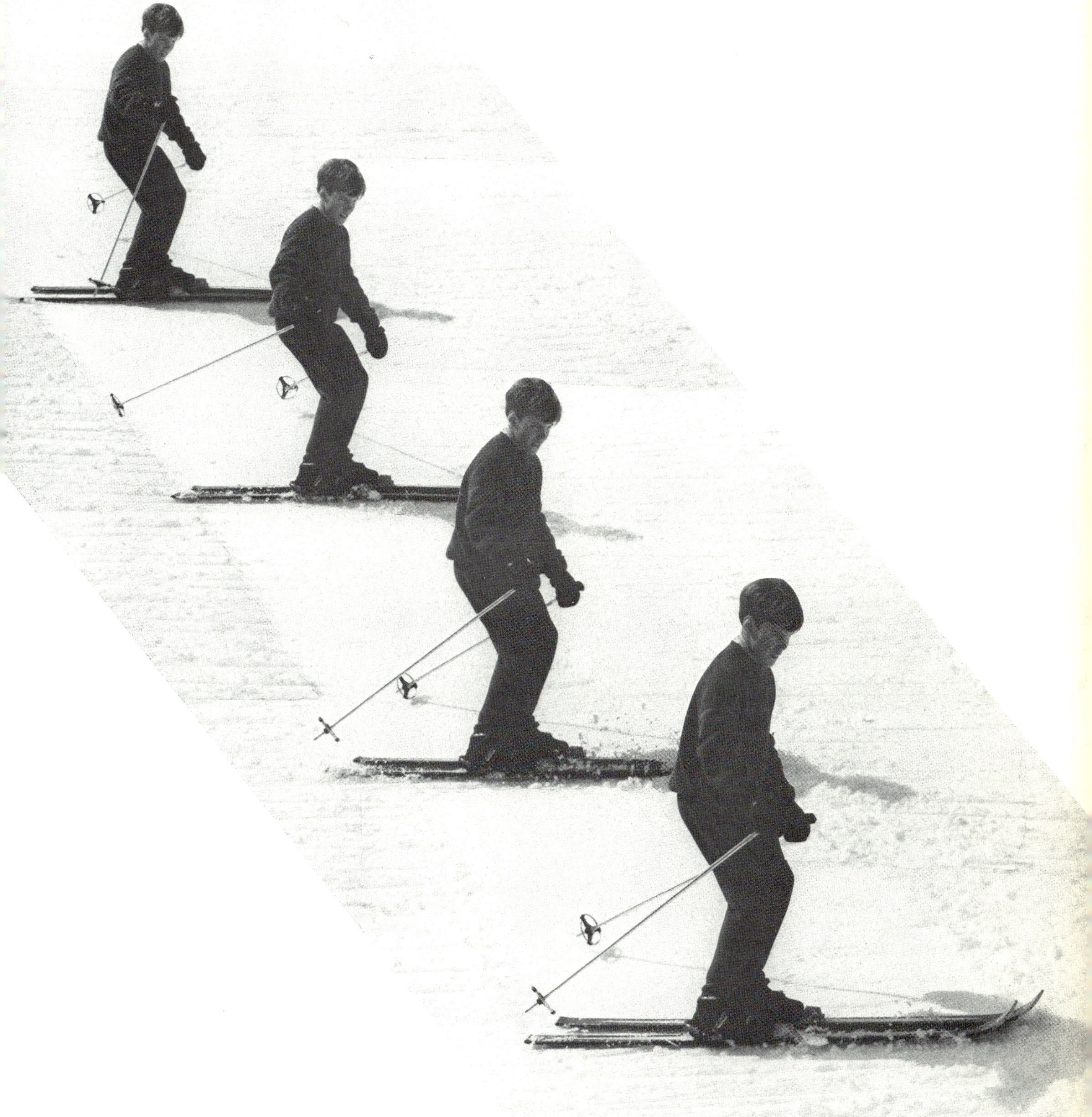

Traversing a fairly steep slope . . .

I flatten my skis . . .

and sideslip . . .

exercise:

Traverse Plus Forward Sideslip

One easy way to practice the forward sideslip is this: Cross the slope in a slow traverse. Rise and at the same time release the grip of the edges by flattening your skis and sideslip diagonally across the slope. It's fun to travel both forward and downhill at the same time and to feel the skis sideslipping under you. Return to a traverse by pressing your knees in toward the slope. This sets your edges. Then rise, flatten the skis and sideslip some more.

If you are having trouble getting the skis to start sideslipping, try a hop—*catlike*—to release your edges.

traverse again . . .

release my edges and sideslip some more.

Starting across in a traverse . . .

I stem the uphill ski . . .

exercise:

Stem to the Forward Sideslip

This exercise, which combines two of the elements you have already learned, trains your reflexes for the christie you are almost ready for.

Crossing the slope in a traverse, stem the uphill ski momentarily *without* shifting your weight onto it. Rise as you slide it back alongside the downhill ski, flattening the skis to release the edges for a forward sideslip, and sink down.

Try this exercise on a right traverse and a left traverse several times each way. Get the feel of: *stem and together, sink and slide.*

and together . . .

sink and . . .

sideslip.

To start the turn . . .

I sink briefly, then . . .

with an up-and-forward motion . . .

The Uphill Christie

Now it's time to put the traverse together with the sideslip. Pick a fairly steep slope. Gather a bit of speed coming across the hill in good traverse position—uphill ski, knee and shoulder ahead. With an up-and-forward motion, release your edges to start your skis sideslipping. As your weight returns to your skis, gradually stop the sideslipping by resetting your edges in a smooth, *catlike* down-motion. At the end of the turn you may find yourself in an uphill traverse. That's why this turn is called an uphill christie.

and rise to a new traverse.

I complete the arc of the uphill christie . . .

followed by a gradual sinking motion . . .

Starting in a snowplow straight down the slope . . .

I transfer my weight to the outside ski.

With an up-and-forward motion, . . .

I bring the inside ski alongside and advanced.

48

The Snowplow Christie

Now you are ready to combine a snowplow turn with an uphill christie. This should be easy for you.

Start down the hill in snowplow position—going easy on the brakes. With an up-and-forward motion, transfer your weight to the ski that is pointed in the direction you want to turn. In the next split second bring the other (inside) ski alongside and slightly advanced. Follow with a smooth sinking motion, as your flexed knees and your hips angle in toward the hill and your upper body tips away from the hill.

At the end of the snowplow christie, rise to the new traverse.

I sink to complete the turn.

Traversing the hill with my weight on the downhill ski . . .

I stem the uphill ski . . .

exercise:

Stem Christie Garlands

Here's a nifty bridge between the uphill christie and the next turn you will learn—the stem christie. This exercise teaches you how to stem and then up-unweight as you quickly close the ski and make both skis sideslip.

Crossing the slope in traverse position, stem the uphill ski briefly. Then, rising up and forward in the same motion, bring the stemmed ski parallel and slightly advanced as you go into a sideslip. *Stem and close and sideslip*—make it all one smooth, fluid action, finishing in a brief sideslip in the same direction you were originally traveling.

briefly, then . . .

*rising up and forward,
I close the uphill ski quickly . . . . .*

*and sink as I sideslip,
then rise to my new traverse.*

Traversing a fairly steep slope . . .

exercise:

Beginning Stem Christie

Here's where you start to put it all together—stem turn, snowplow christie, uphill christie. In this, the beginning stem christie, you wait to bring your skis together until after you have crossed the fall line in the arc of your turn.

Traversing the slope, stem the uphill ski. As you come to the fall line, transfer your weight to the stemmed (outside) ski with a sinking motion of your body. Now rise up and forward, as you bring your *inside* ski parallel. Follow with a smooth down-motion and increased angulation . . .

What's *angulation*? It's the angled position of your entire body over your skis, and it's a lot like making a turn when you're riding a bike. Your forward-flexed knees and hips are pushed *toward* the hill in the skidding arc of the turn, while your upper body is tipped away from the hill. Angulation controls balance while edging your skis.

Practice the beginning stem christie a lot—both to the left and to the right. Each time try to close the skis a little sooner than the time before—but smoothly.

I stem the uphill ski.

I transfer my weight to the outside ski . . .

and close the skis with an up-unweighting . . .

after I cross the fall line . . .

as I complete the arc of the turn.

In a steep traverse . . .

*I sink and stem
the uphill ski, then . . .*

*up and forward, as I transfer my weight
to the outside ski and
quickly bring my inside ski parallel.*

*With my
weight mostly
on my
outside ski . . .*

and my inside ski advanced . . .

*I sink
throughout
the arc of
the turn . . .*

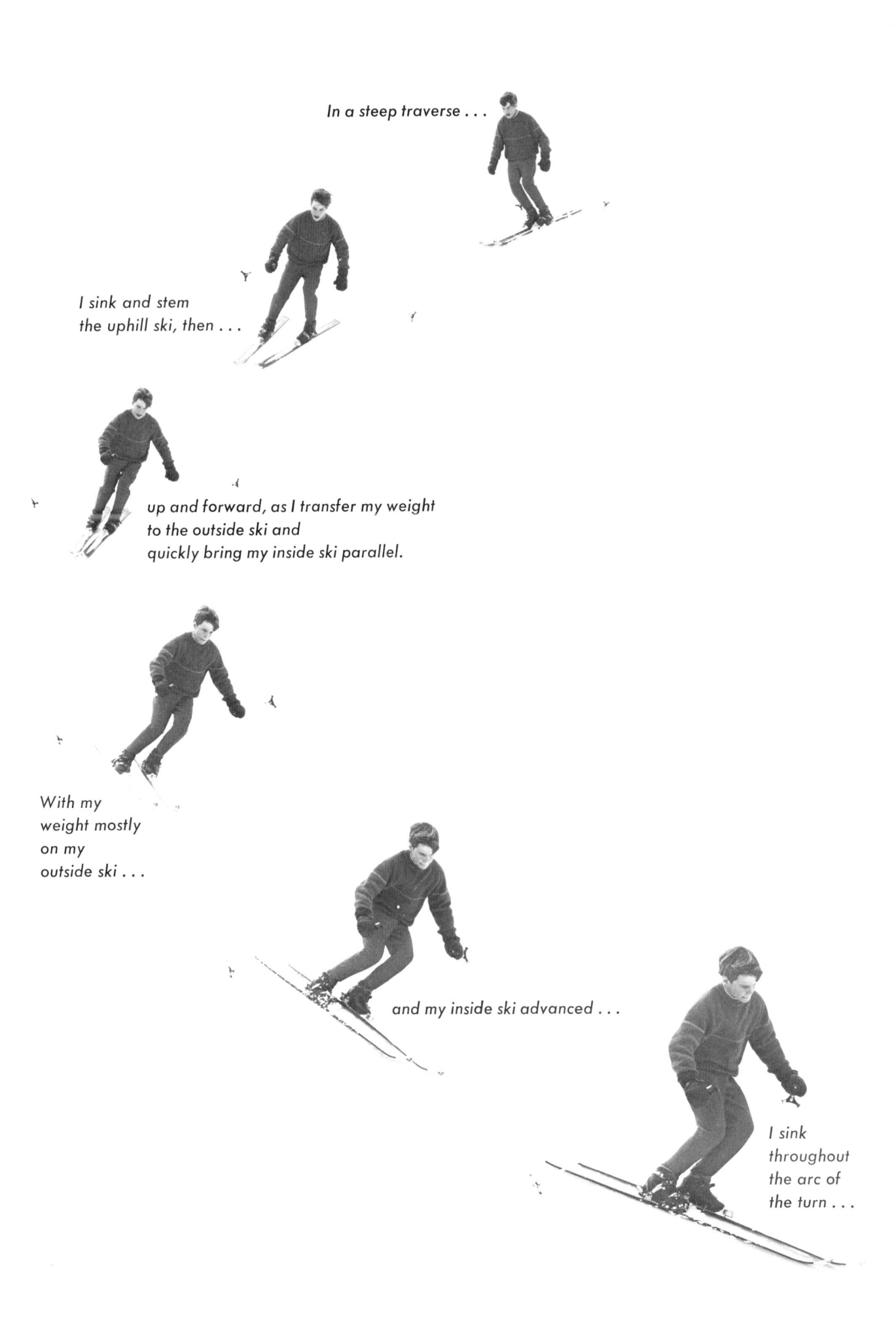

The Stem Christie

Pick a fairly steep slope and start the stem christie in a traverse that points more down the slope than across the slope so that you'll pick up a little speed. You need some speed to take advantage of momentum and gravity to make your skis react properly against the snow in the turn. This is the way it goes:

Moving right along in the traverse, stem your uphill ski briefly, accompanied by a slight sinking of your body. With a smooth up-and-forward motion, transfer your weight to the stemmed (outside) ski and *immediately* bring the unweighted (inside) ski parallel and slightly ahead of the ski your weight is on. As you begin the christie phase of the turn, combine angulation with a gradual sinking motion in your knees. When you have completed the turn, rise to a new traverse.

There are four phases to the stem christie, all flowing smoothly together:

1. Sink and stem the uphill ski
2. Up-unweight to transfer your weight to the outside ski and bring the inside ski parallel
3. Gradually sink forward, keeping your weight on the outside ski throughout the arc of the turn
4. Rise to the new traverse

Practice to complete your *stem-and-together* before the fall line. A very slight, brief stem is all you will need after you get the feel of the stem christie. Connect a lot of them together down the longest slope you can find, traversing only a short distance between each turn.

and begin to rise in a new traverse.

CHRISTIE FROM THE FALL LINE

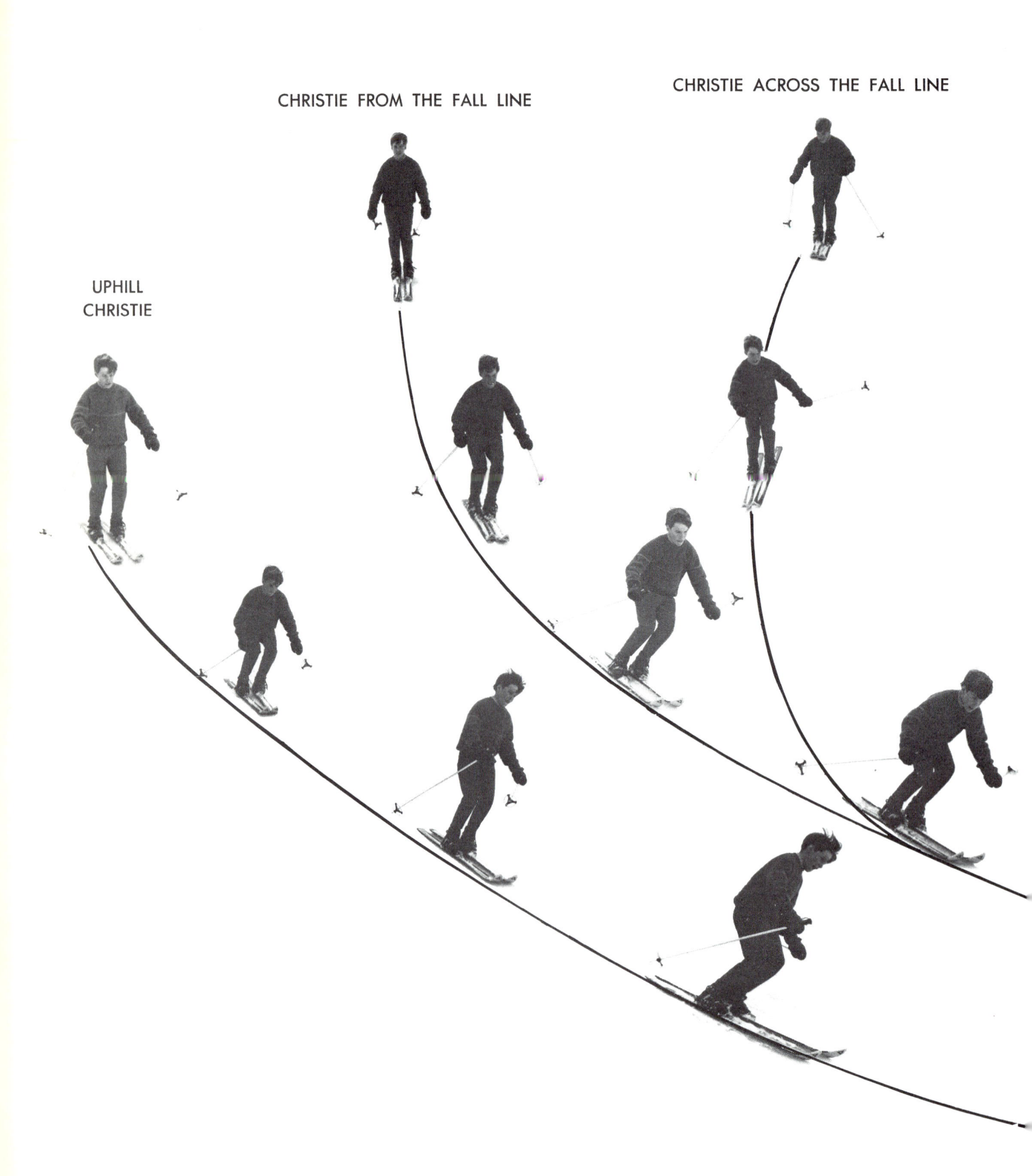

CHRISTIE ACROSS THE FALL LINE

UPHILL
CHRISTIE

exercise:

The Fan

The fan is a sequence of turns for learning to ski parallel.

Start your first run on an oblique angle, half across the slope and half down the slope—and make an uphill christie. Start each of the following runs from higher on the hill, gradually working up to a point where you start a run straight down the fall line—and make a turn. The pictures also show Peter making a turn *across* the fall line, and you can try it too in preparation for what comes next—the parallel christie.

Crossing the slope in a steep traverse...

I sink down and then...

spring up to unweight, so that I can start turning the skis in the new direction.

With my inside ski advanced, I sink down, my weight on my outside ski...

pushing my knees forward and in toward the hill.

My upper body tilts away from the hill...

The Parallel Christie

If you have acquired a good stem christie and if you have practiced closing your skis well before the fall line after a very brief, scant stem, then the parallel christie is going to be easy to learn.

Prepare for the parallel christie with a pronounced down-motion. This is followed by an up-and-forward *catlike* spring to unweight. It enables you, at this unweighted moment, to start the skis turning in the new direction. Immediately transfer your weight to the outside ski. As your parallel christie continues, gradually employ a sinking motion combined with angulation of your body and forward pressure of your knees. These control the arc of the turn and establish your new direction as you rise to a new traverse.

throughout the arc of the turn...

and I rise to a new traverse.

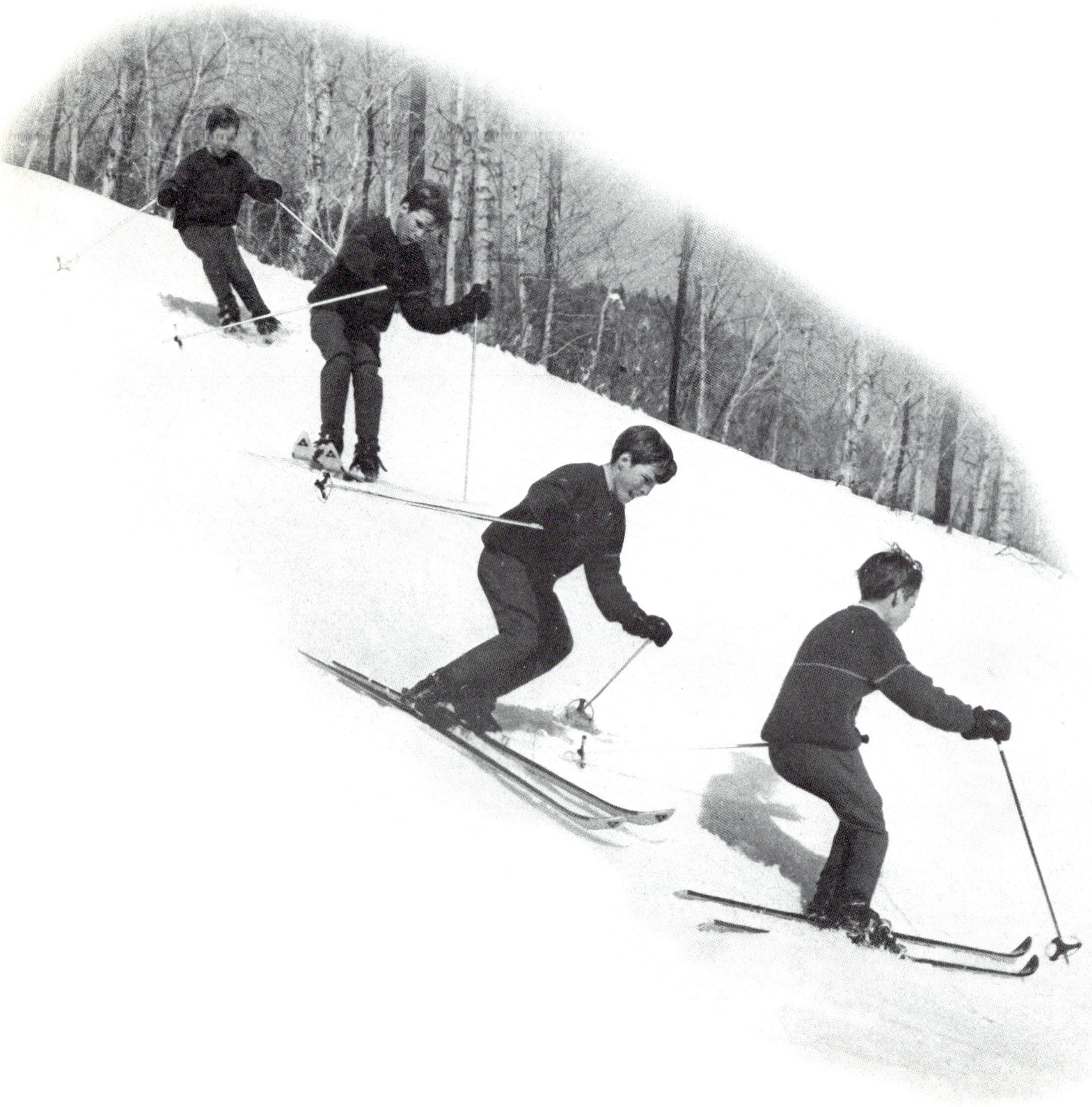

exercise:

Parallel Turn over a Bump

Don't ski *around* every bump in the slope, as so many skiers do. When you see a nice little bump ahead of you, use it. Turn over the top.

Only the middle of Peter's skis are in contact with the snow when he is right on top of the bump. At that exact moment the skis are easy to turn. See how he sinks down across the downhill face of the bump to carve his turn. Notice that he has planted his pole right on top of the bump— and uses it again as he starts another turn farther down the hill.

*Crossing the hill in a traverse,
I see that it's going to get steeper
and decide to slow my speed with a check...*

Parallel with Check

The long looping parallel turns you have learned are fine for a big wide open slope. But now suppose you are traversing back and forth across such a slope and suddenly it narrows to a trail—a trail with a couple of steep pitches in it. What you need is some way of slowing briefly in your traverse before attempting to turn down the hill and back across in the other direction.

Try a *check* before you go into your turn. You have probably seen hockey players "throw a check" when they want to slow their speed abruptly. They simply turn both skates across the direction of flight to put on the brakes. You can do the same thing on skis. Here's how:

You are crossing the slope in a fast traverse. Just before you turn, allow both skis to slide downhill momentarily. Sink in your knees at the same time. Abruptly stop the sliding and plant your downhill pole. That's a check. It puts a sudden temporary platform under you from which to unweight, *catlike,* with a pronounced up-motion. The rest of the turn is merely a parallel turn.

In any parallel turn in which you use it, pole-plant is an important timing factor. The planting of the pole triggers your up-motion; unweighting begins with the pole-plant.

Here I have risen to my new traverse.

I release both skis and let them slide downhill a bit—then, sinking down my knees, abruptly stop the sliding. At the bottom of this down-motion, I plant my pole to trigger the up-motion, as I go ...

upward and forward into the turn, transferring my weight to my outside ski.

Now the skis are tracking in the arc of the turn, my knees and hips angled well to the inside ...

as I sink gradually forward to complete the turn.

The Short Swing

In the American technique, parallel christies tightly linked together with no traverse between are known as short swing. Short swing turns are extremely valuable for skiing steep pitches and drop-offs in narrow trails. They can be done on easy slopes, keeping the skis quite flat, merely brushing the snow from side to side. Or they can be done—as in this series of pictures—with some edge-set on moderately steep slopes. On very steep difficult pitches, they can be a series of hops, the edges set very hard left and right.

On steep slopes you control your skis in the short swing by angulation and edging. The steeper the slope the more pronounced your angulation. Pole-plant becomes a necessity.

These pictures give you the basic idea of the short swing. If you want to learn to do this competently you should probably join an advanced class with a teacher who is a member of the Professional Ski Instructors of America.